HOW TO

BALANCE

YOUR LIFE

HOW TO BALANCE YOUR LIFE

Vie Books is an imprint of Summersdale Publishers Ltd

An Hachette UK Company
www.hachette.co.uk

Summersdale Publishers Ltd
Part of Octopus Publishing Group Limited
Carmelite House
50 Victoria Embankment
LONDON
EC4Y 0DZ
UK

www.summersdale.com

Printed and bound in China

ISBN: 978-1-78685-776-7

Substantial discounts on bulk quantities of Summersdale books are available to corporations, professional associations and other organizations. For details contact general enquiries: telephone: +44 (0) 1243 771107 or email: enquiries@summersdale.com.

Neither the author nor the publisher can be held responsible for any loss or claim arising out of the use, or misuse, of the suggestions made herein. It's always advisable to consult a physician before beginning a new exercise regime or diet.

HOW TO

BALANCE

YOUR LIFE

EVERYDAY TIPS FOR SIMPLER
LIVING AND LASTING HARMONY

ROBIN JAMES

Contents

INTRODUCTION
Finding the right balance

The very fact that you have this book in your hands suggests you feel the need to make a change to your life. If you stop to think about your equilibrium you may find that you are feeling out of kilter. Ask yourself a few basic questions, starting with these: Are you content with your life? Have you got the balance right between home, work and doing the things that are most important to you? Do you pay adequate attention to feeling good and exercising? Do you spend enough time connecting with people, being with loved ones, discovering new things, adventuring or being part of a community and 'giving back'?

You are the only person who can be the judge of that, and what works for you is not something that will necessarily work for others. Once you start asking these sorts of questions it's quite easy to shine a light on areas where you haven't quite got it right and where you need to redress the balance. For instance, it could be that you spend too much time involved in one part of your life while neglecting another.

The aim of this book is to offer some guidance, tips and inspiration on steering yourself back on course to find balance, which in itself will help restore contentment. When you start to feel content about certain aspects of your life, this will positively affect other areas too.

Don't assume that there is an immediate fix or a panacea. Taking things steadily, sorting things out little by little and giving time to embed new ways of behaving rather than rushing headlong into change means there will be a better chance of your new behaviours becoming long-term habits.

Once you find yourself on a more even keel it will be much easier to deal with the unexpected, and it will be easier to right yourself as you continue life's journey.

PART 1

BALANCING YOUR MIND

The best place to begin balancing your life is within you. Achieving a sense of equilibrium will give you the headspace to be able to think clearly about what's important to you. Sometimes this can be as simple as allowing yourself time to stop, pause and take a look at your stress levels. Do you feel like you are travelling through life at top speed, spinning plates and never sufficiently drawing breath? Or are you trudging along feeling demotivated and without clear direction? Wherever you find yourself on this spectrum, now's the opportunity for a fresh start and to find the pace that works best for you.

Find calm

Before you can attempt to think clearly, you need to be calm. This may sound straightforward but it's very likely that day-to-day worries and minor concerns are ever present as "noise" in your subconscious. Try this simple exercise to calm and centre yourself.

Find a quiet and comfortable place to sit, preferably with your bare feet on the ground. If you are indoors, it might help to light a candle as a point of focus.

Plant your feet firmly on the ground, relax your shoulders, place your hands palms down on your legs, keep your back straight and your gaze forward.

Now close your eyes, maintaining the posture, and breathe in. Think only about your breath and the way it feels coming into your body and then out.

Once you are fully aware of your breathing, try taking deeper breaths, breathing in for a count of six and then out for a count of six.

Stay focused on your breath for about five minutes. Your heart rate should now be steady and you should feel relaxed. You are now ready to start thinking clearly.

GIVE YOURSELF HEADSPACE

Stress is a common problem for many of us and affects people in a variety of different ways. The right amount of pressure pushes us to achieve our goals and meet deadlines but, if left unchecked, stress can have a very negative effect. An excess of stress can leave us feeling tired, irritable and even very unwell. As individuals, we all have different needs. This also means that we have different stress factors in our lives. Although we tend to just live with it, there are some simple ways to reduce stress by identifying and controlling the causes. There are several broad factors which would cause stress in anybody, but we know ourselves best and can work out which areas affect us the most. It may be that driving to work makes you stressed, or calling your bank. If so, why not try cycling to work, or talking to someone in person at the local branch of your bank? Identifying these simple triggers and making small changes is the first step to de-stressing your life.

Over the course of two weeks, write down all the things that make you feel stressed, be they places, people or situations. Rate these stresses on a scale from one to ten, with one being only slightly stressful and ten being the most stressful. Once you have identified your high-stress triggers you can take steps to eliminate them.

Think positively

We will all experience difficult situations at some point in our lives, but it's how we deal with them, and not the situations themselves, that has the most impact on our stress levels and resilience. A great way to change your mind about problems is to find a positive within the negative. This can be hard at first, especially in situations that can have quite a strong and lasting effect on your life. Even finding a small positive will make a situation easier to deal with. Perhaps you didn't get the promotion you wanted; maybe it wasn't quite the right time for you, but at least you got the opportunity to think about progressing yourself and moving forward. Perhaps a relationship has ended, but the positive is that you are now free to find someone more suited to you, thereby forming a brighter future. It's not always easy to do this, but the shift in perspective can be very liberating and will stand you in good stead for any challenges ahead.

GET THE PACE RIGHT

To help build a healthier attitude toward yourself, the first thing to do is to simply slow down. Many of us are living our lives at an ever-faster pace, and trying to balance a whole range of commitments from work to personal interests to relationships. This can leave us feeling stressed and frustrated when we are forced to stop, for instance when we have to wait for something. Combat this by taking those moments when your bus is late, or when you are stuck in traffic, to do something relaxing like deep breathing or listening to music.

While it may seem counter-intuitive, slowing down will boost your productivity levels. A study published in *Psychological Science* suggests that taking time to sit and do nothing at some point in the day – to simply take stock of a situation – will increase your commitment to your goals, increasing the likelihood of achieving your targets.

A 2009 study from University College London examined the behaviours of 96 people over the space of 12 weeks, and found that the average time it takes for a new habit to stick is 66 days. To feel more motivated and energized each day means changing your way of living, which will take time and persistence. Embracing longer timelines, as well as being more realistic, will help you feel more positive if you don't immediately achieve your goals.

AUDIT
YOUR
LIFE

Write a list or make a chart using the headings "I'm happy with the status quo", "I'm not really happy" and "This could be better" to note down areas of your life that might need to be addressed. Write down a wide variety of ideas, in whichever order they pop into your head, and position them under one of the headings according to how you feel about them. This simple exercise gives you a starting point and helps you separate out your thoughts rather than seeing your concerns as one impenetrable block. Once you've put things in writing you can begin to prioritize areas of your life and begin to find balance.

I'M HAPPY WITH THE STATUS QUO	I'M NOT REALLY HAPPY	THIS COULD BE BETTER

FIND TIME TO TRULY RELAX

The breathing exercise on page ten is a quick and simple way to calm yourself, and is a technique that can be used on a day-to-day basis, particularly in times of stress. However, it's a very useful practice to actively take time out on a regular basis to experience deep relaxation. There are a number of ways in which this can be achieved.

MINDFULNESS

Most of us find it hard to close out the constant "noise" of life – the things that chew away at you as worries or stresses. The practice of mindfulness is about taking time to be present and to experience life as it unfolds moment by moment. Find a quiet spot if you can, take in your surroundings and become aware of the place you are sitting in – listen to the sounds around you and notice what thoughts are in your mind. This simple step is called orienting and is the first stepping stone to finding calm. Next, apply the same breathing technique from page ten. Try to think only about your breathing, and if unwanted thoughts pop into your head just refocus on the breath entering and leaving your body. You'll notice that your heart rate slows and you start to feel more relaxed. Once you are in this state, try to maintain it for as long as you can and don't rush straight back into whatever it was you were doing previously. When you're ready, take time to emerge from this very relaxed state and re-join the flow of your day with calmness.

APPLIED RELAXATION

Sometimes when you're in a stressful
situation it's hard to find a way forward
or to release yourself from an anxious state.
Like mindfulness, this technique works by drawing
your focus toward something very specific, in this case it
involves learning to relax the muscles in the body individually
to help you feel calmer. For best effects, you should carry out
this exercise lying stretched out on the floor. Extend your toes
and raise your feet off the ground by stretching your ankles, your
calves and your quads. Continue this process until every muscle in
your body is stretching, literally from head to toe. Hold the stretch
briefly and then drop it and relax. You may need to practise a
few times to get the hang of it, but once you've learned how
to do this you can use the technique to help you stay calm
the next time a stressful situation arises. If you are in
a situation where lying on the floor is inappropriate,
try simply clenching and releasing your fists.

MEDITATION

Meditation has been used by many cultures around the world for centuries. Yoga and t'ai chi are both described as "moving meditation", which shows that this practice takes many forms. You don't necessarily have to sit cross-legged and chant mantras to meditate, though you can if this is something you find helpful.

Put simply, meditation is a way of quietening your mind and allowing yourself time to be still. A good way to start, if meditation is new to you, is to sit in a comfortable position with a straight back, resting your hands palms up in your lap. Close your eyes and focus on one of your other senses, such as your hearing. When your mind begins to wander, gently bring it back to your chosen sense. Doing this for five to ten minutes can make a huge difference to your day.

Creative visualization

Creative visualization is a technique practised by many as a means of literally "seeing" where you want to be to help you reach that end goal. It is easy to be put off by the "what-ifs" that a situation might bring to mind, and this is where creative visualization can help.

Find a comfortable chair to sit in, and relax.

Begin by closing your eyes and focusing on the natural rhythm of your breathing.

Start to build up a picture in your head of how a happier, more content you would look and behave. Where are you? Who is beside you in this happy place?

Notice every detail and enjoy how it feels.

While you are working on becoming happier with your life, carry this mental image with you as inspiration.

AFFIRMATIONS

An affirmation is a positive phrase that you use to help change negative beliefs to positive ones. They work well both when written down and when said out loud. A positive affirmation to help you change your attitude to stressful situations could be:

I FEEL BALANCED AND HAPPY.

OR

I SOLVE MY PROBLEMS QUICKLY AND EFFECTIVELY.

It is important that the affirmation focuses on the positive outcome that you want rather than the negative possibility that you wish to avoid, and that it is written or spoken in the present tense.

Sound bathing

Many of the relaxation techniques in this book can be achieved in the comfort of your own home, but if you feel like trying something different there are all sorts of guided options available. The ancient Tibetan practice of sound bathing involves lying in a dimly lit room and listening to soothing sounds played on special bowls made from metal and crystal. Research shows that hearing certain sounds reduces the level of the stress hormone cortisol, and taking a sound bath can lower your blood pressure, reduce anxiety levels and improve your mood.

PART 2

KEEPING FIT
AND HEALTHY

It's often easy to forget about how our bodies feel when we are so preoccupied with what's going on in our heads. A body audit can be a useful process for discovering which areas of your life lack balance. Consider your personal well-being and ask yourself these questions:

Am I in good physical shape?

Am I happy with my overall health?

Am I happy with my body weight?

Do I treat my body with respect?

Do I do enough exercise?

Do I eat healthily?

FIND THE
RIGHT
EXERCISE
FOR YOU

Have you ever noticed how good you feel after a swim, a brisk walk or a jog? It's the release of the "happy" chemicals endorphins and dopamine, and the reduction in the stress hormones cortisol and adrenalin, that make you feel so good. According to research, just 20 minutes of exercise can boost your mood for up to 12 hours. The tips on the following pages will help you to get moving and start feeling the mood-boosting benefits of regular exercise.

EXERCISES FOR BEGINNERS

Whether physical exercise is not on your agenda or you are a total addict, there's a lot you can do at home. If you are in a sedentary job and at a desk for much of the day, or if you spend hours relaxing in front of the TV, there are some simple exercises that you can perform, which, over time, will help improve your flexibility and balance. Try the following set of exercises as a starting point. You will need to be sitting on a stable chair with no wheels or arms.

Neck stretches

Sit with your feet flat on the floor, hip-width apart and your back leaning flat against the chair. Bend your elbow and place your hand on top of the opposite shoulder and press down on it. Tilt your head away from your hand. Hold this stretch for five seconds and repeat on the other side. Repeat another two times on each side.

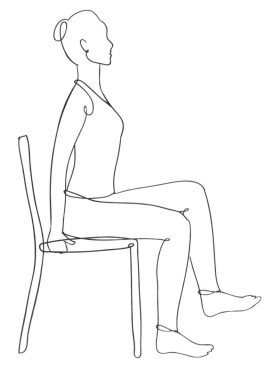

Seated knee lift

Sit with your feet flat on the floor and your back straight and unsupported. Hold the sides of the chair with your hands for support. Lift your right leg as far as it feels comfortable and then lower it with control – try to complete the lift five times. Switch sides and repeat with the left leg for five repetitions. This exercise stretches your hip rotators.

If you want to give your hamstrings a stretch too, perform the seated knee lift but after lifting your leg, try straightening it out until you can feel a nice behind your knee. Slowly bend your leg and gently lower it to the floor.

Ankle and hamstring stretch

Remain seated in your chair but lean your back against the back support for this exercise (you can hold the sides of the chair for some extra support if desired). Raise your right leg off the ground in front of you and start by flexing your ankle so your toes are pointing up at the sky. Hold for a few seconds – you should feel a pull on your hamstrings – and then point the foot so your ankle is elongated. In the process of flexing and pointing your feet, try to think about going through your foot one section at a time so that you are using and strengthening all your muscles in that region. Hold your leg with a pointed foot for a few seconds and then repeat the movement another four times with the same foot. Lower the right leg and repeat on the other side.

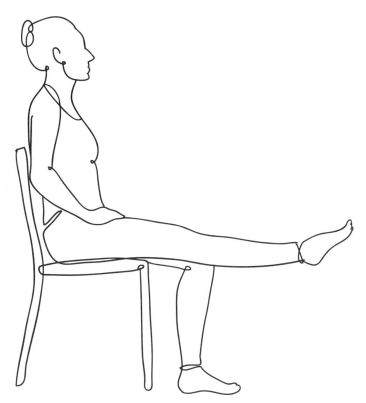

AEROBIC EXERCISE

If you want to start feeling fitter and healthier, gentle aerobic exercise is the best way to begin. Here are some of the most popular physical activities that people partake in for fitness and well-being.

Walk

Walking is such a simple form of exercise and it can be incorporated into your daily life with ease. Adding regular walking into your routine will keep you fitter and healthier and can reduce feelings of anxiety as it will help your body produce serotonin. Even if you lead a very busy life, walking can fit in to your routine. Try parking further from the office, taking the stairs rather than the elevator, or going for a brisk 15-minute walk at lunchtime. It is a healthy habit to form and you will soon be reaping the benefits. Once you are comfortable with these short walks, increase their length and try using walking poles. The arm movement associated with the use of walking poles adds intensity, which helps to burn more calories. The other benefits of using walking poles is that they improve balance and stability, helping to maintain good posture, especially in the upper back.

Swim

Swimming is one of the best forms of exercise, both in terms of giving you a full-body workout, which leaves you tired for the right reasons, and in allowing you to relax and unwind. The rhythmic lap of the water with each stroke and the focus on your technique and breathing really makes this a great way to move your mind away from the stresses of your day. Add to that the fact that floating in water is a wonderfully calming experience and you've got a perfect recipe for relaxation.

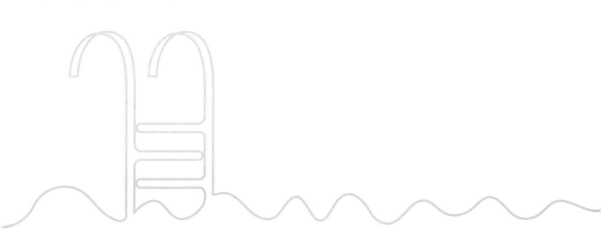

Run

Running is cheap compared to other sports and fitness regimes, as well as being convenient. "Couch to 5k" and other initiatives have made this sport so much more accessible, and the health benefits are significant: regular running will help you burn fat and maintain a healthy weight; it also promotes a healthy heart, lowers blood pressure and is hugely beneficial for your mental health. The UK-based mental health charity Mind has stated that switching from a sedentary lifestyle to doing cardiovascular exercise at least three times a week can reduce depression by up to 20 per cent due to the release of endorphins, the body's feel-good chemicals.

Yoga

Yoga is an ancient form of exercise that originates from India. It has become very popular in recent years, and with good reason. As well as being a calming form of exercise, it can also be very good for releasing stress from the body. Yoga combines movements with breathing to help the mind focus on what the body is doing. This physical focus helps you to relax and stop thinking about the worries of the day. Why not try a class local to you, or look for tutorials online?

To start, here are some yoga poses to incorporate into your daily life:

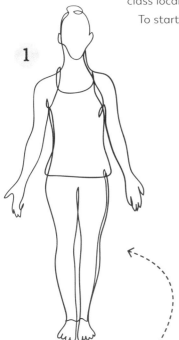

From Mountain pose move into **Standing Half Forward Bend**. Stretch your arms up on the exhale. Engage your legs and bend your torso forward on the hinge of your hips to form a flat back. Be still in Standing Half Forward Bend to strengthen your back while stimulating your internal organs. Hold the pose for three in and out breaths.

Whenever you find yourself standing still, practise **Mountain**. Inhale: engage your legs and thighs, stabilize your core, lift through your chest. Exhale: roll your shoulders back and pull them down the spine.

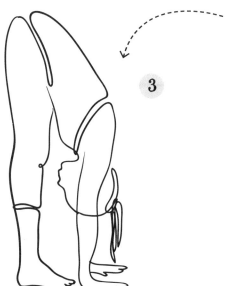

Move into **Standing Full Forward Bend** by first bending your knees slightly, ensuring feet are together, before extending your arms to touch your toes, or as near as is comfortable. Resting your hands on a block just in front of your toes is sometimes useful for this pose to avoid overstretching. Press your torso against your thighs, allowing your head to hang. Take deep breaths and slightly lengthen the torso each time for a deeper stretch.

3

From a Standing Full Forward Bend, inhale and lift your torso parallel to the earth, rest your palms on your shins or your thighs. Hold. Release the position as you exhale. Then return to Mountain pose.

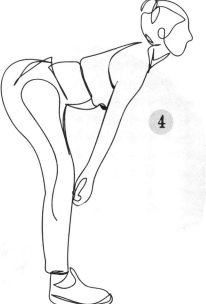

4

Strengthen your arms and shoulders in **Plank**. Lie on your front, ensuring your wrists are below your shoulders and your feet are either hip-distance apart or big toes and heels touching. Maintain a straight line between your back and your legs and lift your body off the mat. Hold and take mindful breaths while in the position. Build your stamina by holding the pose a little longer each day.

Give a powerful stretch to the whole body in **Downward Dog**. Start in Plank. Inhale. As you exhale, lift your tail bone skyward, push back away from your hands and bring your heels toward the ground.

Breathe in before going into a **Lunge** position to encourage muscle relief in your groin and thighs. Start on all fours, with your wrists under your shoulders, knees under your hips and wrists in line with your ankles. Inhale: bring your left foot between your hands, with toes and fingertips in line. Exhale: look forward and up to keep the shoulders from rounding forward and let your hips sink a little lower, without pushing all your weight into your lower back. If you can, rest your hands on your knee for a deeper stretch. Repeat on the other side.

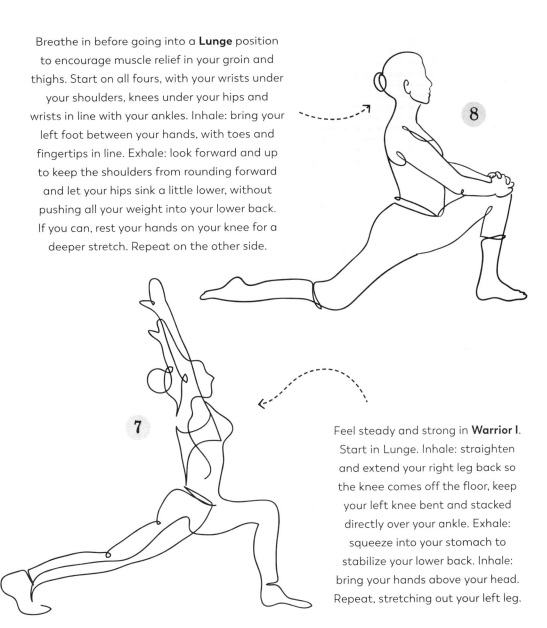

8

7

Feel steady and strong in **Warrior I**. Start in Lunge. Inhale: straighten and extend your right leg back so the knee comes off the floor, keep your left knee bent and stacked directly over your ankle. Exhale: squeeze into your stomach to stabilize your lower back. Inhale: bring your hands above your head. Repeat, stretching out your left leg.

9

Connect with your inner spirit in **Warrior II**.
Start in Mountain (see page 36). Inhale: step back
with your left foot and pivot it slightly, so that your
toes are facing away from you. Exhale: bend your
right knee and stack it directly above your ankle.
Inhale. Exhale: extend your right arm forward, your
left arm behind, keeping them parallel to the floor.
Keep your torso lifted and arms straight. Hold for as
long as you feel strong. Repeat on the other side.

Sit in **Staff** to lengthen your hamstrings and to improve your posture. Sit with both legs extended out in front of you. Inhale: use your hands to pull the flesh of your buttocks away from your tail bone to connect your "sit bones" to the ground. Exhale: lengthen your spine and place your palms on the ground.

Invigorate your energy flow in **Seated Forward Bend**. Begin in Staff (see page 40). Inhale: raise your hands above your head. Exhale: hinge from the hips and fold forward, keeping your spine straight. Depending on your flexibility, hold your shins, ankles or toes and breathe for as long as you feel comfortable.

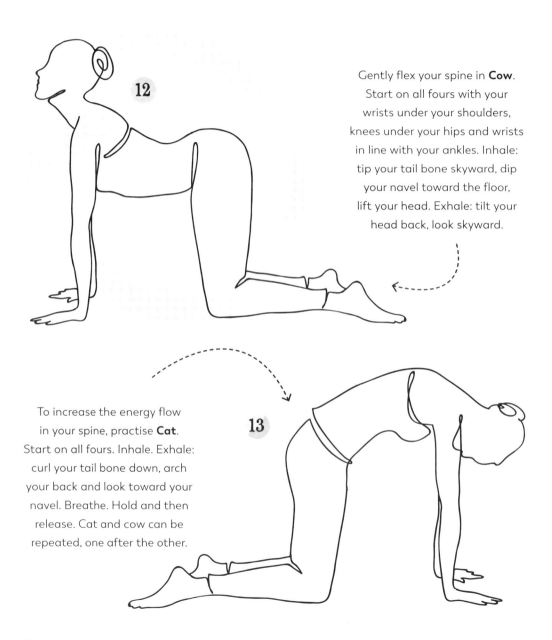

12

Gently flex your spine in **Cow**. Start on all fours with your wrists under your shoulders, knees under your hips and wrists in line with your ankles. Inhale: tip your tail bone skyward, dip your navel toward the floor, lift your head. Exhale: tilt your head back, look skyward.

To increase the energy flow in your spine, practise **Cat**. Start on all fours. Inhale. Exhale: curl your tail bone down, arch your back and look toward your navel. Breathe. Hold and then release. Cat and cow can be repeated, one after the other.

13

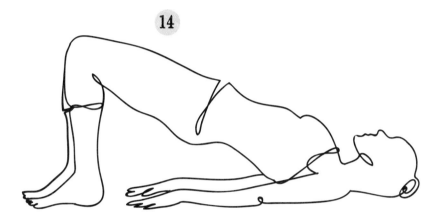

14

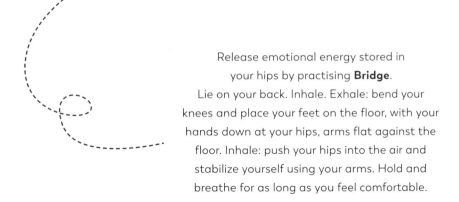

Release emotional energy stored in
your hips by practising **Bridge**.
Lie on your back. Inhale. Exhale: bend your
knees and place your feet on the floor, with your
hands down at your hips, arms flat against the
floor. Inhale: push your hips into the air and
stabilize yourself using your arms. Hold and
breathe for as long as you feel comfortable.

Eat well

When we are making an effort to change areas of our lifestyle, eating is usually a major point of focus. We often have a strange relationship with food and consider "treating" ourselves with those foodstuffs that are usually not good for us. With the help of the advertising industry, we are led to believe that we will find comfort in sugary confections, high-fat foods or alcohol. Yes, instant satisfaction can be found in this way, but why not try turning the dial to a different mindset and consider "treating" yourself by giving your body the benefits of nutrients that will actually help it?

Start your good-eating journey by aiming for a balanced diet. This means eating the right amount of calories for your age, height and sex, and ensuring you get enough protein, healthy fats, fibre and vitamin-rich fruits and vegetables to give you a sound basis for general health and good digestion. Eating a balanced diet can put you in the best shape to stave off stress and illness, and it is as an excellent starting point for lasting good health.

Avoid "going on a diet" as many "diets" aim for speedy weight loss and can often be unsustainable. Plus, they generally make you feel restricted in your eating and have the counter-effect of leaving you craving unhealthy food.

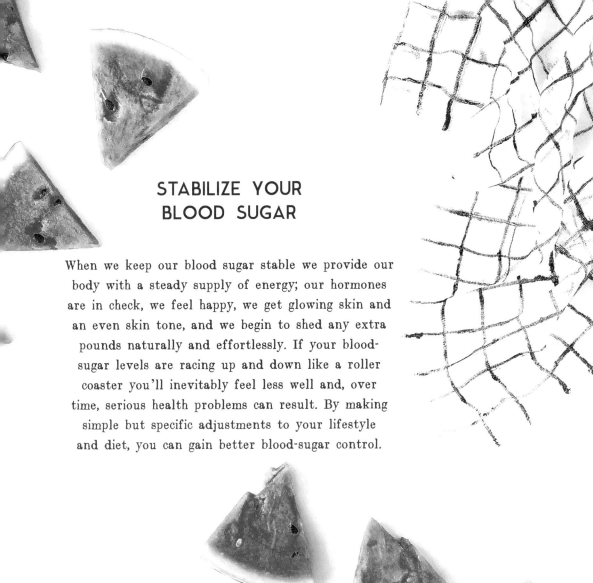

STABILIZE YOUR
BLOOD SUGAR

When we keep our blood sugar stable we provide our
body with a steady supply of energy; our hormones
are in check, we feel happy, we get glowing skin and
an even skin tone, and we begin to shed any extra
pounds naturally and effortlessly. If your blood-
sugar levels are racing up and down like a roller
coaster you'll inevitably feel less well and, over
time, serious health problems can result. By making
simple but specific adjustments to your lifestyle
and diet, you can gain better blood-sugar control.

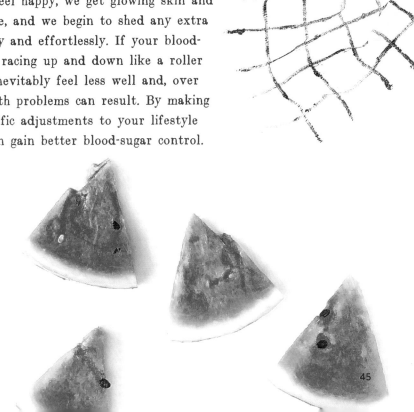

EVEN OUT YOUR EATING

It's important to spread out your daily food intake, starting with breakfast. Consuming more food in just one or two meals a day causes greater fluctuations in blood-sugar levels. Instead, aim to eat three healthy meals a day with two nutritious snacks, such as a handful of nuts or carrot sticks dipped in hummus, to help maintain stable blood sugar.

KEEP YOUR GI LOW

GI stands for glycaemic index. This is a measurement of how much energy a food will give you from sugars. High-GI foods tend to be things like sweets and pastries, while vegetables and lean protein such as fish, skinless chicken and tofu have a low GI. A low-GI diet can have many health benefits, including aiding weight loss, and is particularly good for combating stress. High-GI foods will cause a spike in blood sugar, which will then drop rapidly, leaving you feeling tired, irritable and hungry again. This is the perfect formula for feeling stressed. Low-GI foods, on the other hand, help keep blood-sugar levels more steady, avoiding those dips and helping you feel calmer.

EAT ENOUGH GOOD FATS

Although we are often told that eating a low-fat diet is healthy, certain fats are needed for optimum health. In fact, certain fats help ensure your brain and immune system function properly. Making sure you include some of these good fats in your diet can help to reduce the negative effects of stress on your body, and help your body to cope better with stress.

The four main types of fat are monounsaturated, polyunsaturated, saturated and trans. It is the first two types of fat that you need in your diet, and these can be found in foods such as fish, nuts, seeds, olive oil and avocados.

ACE

Aim to eat plenty of foods rich in vitamins A, C and E. These antioxidants help regulate the body and reduce inflammation, while boosting immunity.

Vitamin A is found in the form of retinol in products such as fish liver oil and egg yolks. Too much retinol can be bad for the health though, so balance this with beta-carotene, found in mainly yellow and orange fruits and vegetables, such as carrots, butternut squash and apricots. Vitamin C is found in good amounts in citrus fruits, broccoli, berries and tomatoes, and vitamin E is found in nuts, seeds, avocados, olive oil and wheatgerm. Adding some of these foods to your diet could make you feel healthier and happier.

Less salt

Being stressed can make us crave salt, as our adrenal glands become exhausted and are unable to make adrenaline and cortisol. This results in a salt imbalance, which makes it very easy to reach for salty foods – especially as many of these foods are also fatty and comforting. Although a high salt intake alone does not increase stress levels, the associated health problems such as weight gain and high blood pressure certainly do, so give salt a wide berth. Instead, choose fruit as a snack and prepare your meals from fresh produce, as pre-packaged foods are usually very high in salt.

Get a B-vit boost

The B-vitamin group is particularly important for maintaining a healthy balanced diet and keeping stress at bay. Among their other functions, B vitamins are involved in the body's control of tryptophan, a building block for serotonin. Too little tryptophan can lead to a drop in serotonin, which can lead to a low mood. The main vitamins to pay attention to are B1, B2, B3, B5, B6, B7, B9 and B12, all of which can be found in a balanced diet, especially in foods such as spinach, broccoli, asparagus and liver. If you eat a lot of processed foods, or are a vegan, you may be lacking in certain B vitamins, in which case adding a B-vitamin supplement to your diet can have an excellent effect.

MAKE A GOOD
START TO THE DAY

A common misconception is that you'll lose weight if you skip breakfast. In fact, the opposite is true. To keep you going until lunchtime, try having porridge, high-fibre cereals, wholemeal toast, poached or boiled eggs. Turn to the following pages for some healthy breakfast recipes to try.

Bircher muesli
(or overnight oats)

This breakfast is super-simple to make and keeps for up to four days in the fridge, so you could double or triple this recipe and make a small batch each time.

SERVES 1

PREPARATION TIME

5 minutes

COOKING TIME

None, but must be left overnight in the fridge.

INGREDIENTS

100 ml (3 ½ fl oz) milk
– dairy, soya or nut
100 g (3 ½ oz) porridge oats
100 ml (3 ½ fl oz)
natural yoghurt
25 g (1 oz) mixed nuts, roughly
chopped (such as almonds,
pecans or hazelnuts) (optional)
1 tsp chia seeds
Fresh banana or
berries, to serve

Optional extras:
Pumpkin seeds, sunflower
seeds, a spoonful of
nut butter, flaked nuts,
granola, honey, sliced
apple and cinnamon

METHOD

Add the ingredients to a clean jam jar and mix together.

Screw on the lid and place in the fridge overnight.

Add some mashed-up banana and berries, or any optional extras, to the top of your breakfast before eating.

SOFT-BOILED EGGS WITH ASPARAGUS SOLDIERS

This breakfast is easy to make and very balanced. It's a great way to start the day and something the whole family can enjoy.

SERVES 4

PREPARATION TIME

5 minutes

COOKING TIME

8 minutes

INGREDIENTS

1 large bunch of
asparagus (approx.
12 spears)
8 slices pancetta
4 large eggs
4 slices sourdough bread
Salt and pepper for
seasoning

METHOD

Wash the asparagus and trim off the woody ends.

Heat a griddle pan on the hob and a separate saucepan containing water to boil.

Slice the pancetta into 12 strips. Then wrap each asparagus spear with a strip of pancetta. Place the spears on the hot griddle, turning them occasionally so they're evenly cooked and the pancetta has crisp edges.

Meanwhile, place the eggs in the boiling water and cook for five minutes. Then place into egg cups.

Toast the bread slices and slice into soldiers, arranging them beside the eggs and asparagus spears.

Snack carefully

Banish cakes, sweets and salty snacks that are high in sugar and salt but low in energy, and switch to snacks such as nuts, seeds, raisins and fruit. For example, a great slow-release energy combination is a mid-morning banana with a handful of nuts. You'll notice a difference and feel fuller for longer. You could also try these simple, healthy snack ideas.

TRAIL MIX

This is a great low-carb go-to for when you feel the urge to snack. Keep a small bowl on your desk at work to graze on instead of reaching for sugary snacks.

PREPARATION TIME

5 minutes

INGREDIENTS

300 g (11 oz) unsalted peanuts
300 g (11 oz) whole almonds
300 g (11 oz) toasted pumpkin seeds
50 g (2 oz) coconut chips
150 g (5 oz) raisins or sultanas

METHOD

Mix the ingredients together and take a small handful whenever you feel your energy levels dipping.

Store in an airtight container and consume within two weeks.

Hummus

This is a great dip that goes perfectly with celery, cucumber, bell peppers and carrots.

SERVES 4 as a starter

PREPARATION TIME

5 minutes

INGREDIENTS

400 g (14 oz) canned chickpeas
1 small clove of garlic
1 tbsp tahini
1 lemon
1 tbsp extra virgin olive oil
Sea salt to season
A selection of raw vegetables
sliced into sticks for dipping
4 wholemeal pitta breads

Optional extras:
Paprika
A sprig of fresh parsley

METHOD

Drain the chickpeas and pour them into a food processor.

Peel and add the garlic, then add the tahini, a good squeeze of lemon juice and a tablespoon of oil.

Season with a pinch of sea salt, pop the lid on and blitz until smooth, stopping midway if you need to scrape down the hummus from the sides.

Have a taste and add more lemon juice or a splash of water to loosen, if needed, then transfer to a serving dish.

Serve with sliced raw vegetables, such as carrots, cucumbers, radishes or bell peppers, and some warm wholemeal pitta bread. Sprinkle paprika and fresh parsley on top before serving.

RAW ENERGY BALLS

You'll get around 15 small but mighty balls from this recipe. Full of natural sugars, protein and fibre, they'll boost you throughout your day.

MAKES 15 balls

PREPARATION TIME

15 minutes

COOKING TIME

No cooking, but 15 minutes chilling time.

INGREDIENTS

55 g (2 oz) dark chocolate
220 g (8 oz) dates
3 tbsp peanut butter
1 tbsp chia seeds
160 g (6 oz) rolled oats
50 g flaked almonds

METHOD

Grate the chocolate or break it into squares, depending on whether you'd prefer choc chips or an even chocolatey texture.

Blitz together all ingredients in a blender (if you prefer chocolate chips stir these in at the end) until they make a thick paste.

Roll into spheres the size of ping-pong balls. Then roll them in flaked almonds.

They are ready to eat straight away but 15 minutes in the fridge will help firm up the mixture. The perfect compromise is to snack on one while the rest cool in the fridge.

REDCURRANT SMOOTHIE

Smoothies are a great way of using up excess soft fruits.
Be creative and experiment with different flavour combinations.

SERVES 2

PREPARATION TIME

5 minutes

INGREDIENTS

240 g (8 oz) redcurrants, fresh or frozen
1 small banana, peeled
5 tbsp blackcurrant and apple cordial
240 ml (8 fl oz) natural yogurt
Redcurrants and fresh mint leaves to garnish

METHOD

Remove any stalks from the redcurrants.

Place the redcurrants, banana, cordial and yogurt in a blender and blend on high speed for a minute or two.

If you are using frozen redcurrants the smoothie will be a good temperature but if you are using fresh redcurrants you may want to chill before consuming.

Sprinkle a few redcurrants and mint leaves on top of the smoothie to serve.

EATING PLANS FOR A BALANCED DIET

Try to start being more mindful about what you are eating. Here are some menu ideas that will prevent your energy levels from dipping and leading you to indulge in unhealthy snacking. Recipes for these are readily available on the internet or in good recipe books. Don't forget to drink plenty of water before mealtimes and chew slowly while you eat to encourage feelings of fullness.

BREAKFAST IDEAS

- Sugar-free cereal and a small 120 ml (4 fl oz) glass of juice.

- Wholemeal toast and peanut butter.

- Porridge topped with fresh fruit.

- Smoothie (p.62).

- Poached eggs on granary toast followed by half a grapefruit.

- Bircher muesli (p.52)

MID-MORNING OR
AFTERNOON SNACK IDEAS

- A handful of nuts or coconut flakes.

- A hard-boiled egg.

- A small dish of olives.

- A piece of cheese.

- A slice of smoked salmon.

- A handful of celery sticks dipped in nut butter.

- Raw vegetables with hummus (p.58) or guacamole.

- Energy balls (p.60)

Lunch ideas

- Leftover cold meat, such as chicken drumsticks, dipped in mustard.

- Mini salad of mozzarella, tomatoes, basil leaves and olive oil.

- Canned tuna or sardines with mashed avocado on sourdough toast.

- Salad using a variety of salad leaves, roasted vegetables, protein (e.g. fish, meat, cheese, nuts, seeds, boiled eggs) and a dressing.

- Mixed vegetable soup with added protein for a topping (e.g. meat, fish, chickpeas, grated parmesan).

- Wraps or sandwiches with fillings such as roasted vegetables, spinach, guacamole and feta or goat's cheese, salad leaves, chicken, harissa mayonnaise, hummus (p.58), grated carrot, pine nuts or coriander and rocket (arugula).

- Vegetable frittata and salad.

Dinner ideas

- Baked potato or sweet potato with a tasty topping – such as hummus and parsley, chicken and homemade coleslaw or flaked mackerel and lemon crème fraiche – paired with a leafy green salad.

- Wholemeal pasta, tuna and tomato bake.

- Brown rice risotto or paella (you can play about with traditional recipes to add and take away elements of your choice).

- Noodle stir-fry using a variety of vegetables and proteins (e.g. meat, fish or vegan substitutes).

- Lentil and vegetable casserole (sausage or chorizo can be added to these if you prefer to include meat).

MODERATE

CAFFEINE

Many of us rely on that first cup of coffee in the morning to wake us up, or a cup of tea to keep us going at midday, but these caffeinated drinks, along with cola and foods containing caffeine, such as chocolate, could be having an adverse effect on your stress levels – perhaps the opposite effect to the one you intend.

Drinking a caffeinated drink can make us feel more alert because it induces the initial stages of the stress reaction, boosting cortisol production. Consuming large quantities of caffeine, however, can cause the exhaustion phase of stress. Added to this, caffeine can be very addictive and stopping suddenly can cause withdrawal symptoms. Try cutting down slowly to no more than 300 mg of caffeine in a day – that's the equivalent of three cups of coffee or four cups of tea. Have fun experimenting with the huge variety of herbal teas available on the market to fill the gap, or try a non-caffeinated version.

ALCOHOL

After a hard day at work, many people will reach for a drink to help them relax. Alcohol does have a calming effect, but this is negated by its depressant qualities and the feeling of anxiety that can be left behind once the effects wear off. Alcohol can also disturb sleep, contrary to the popular idea of it being a "nightcap".

Try to cut down drinking alcohol as much as possible and, if you do go for a tipple, opt for a small glass of Chianti, Merlot or Cabernet Sauvignon, as the grape skins used in these wines are rich with the sleep hormone, melatonin. All good things in moderation, though!

Mocktail recipes

If you've decided to cut down on alcohol or go alcohol-free, try these delicious and healthy mocktail recipes that will leave you feeling fresh the next morning.

VIRGIN WATERMELON MARGARITA

SERVES 4

INGREDIENTS

1 medium watermelon, cut into chunks
100 ml (4 fl oz) fresh lime juice (about 3–4 limes)
4 tsp agave syrup
80 ml (3 fl oz) sparking water
6–8 mint leaves, to garnish

METHOD

In a blender, puree the watermelon chunks in stages and decant the juice into cups.

Repeat the process until you have four cups of watermelon puree.

Pour the puree into a large bowl, add the lime juice and agave syrup and stir until mixed through.

Transfer the juice between four large wine glasses so they're three-quarters full and top up with sparkling water. Stir briefly then serve, garnished with mint if desired.

COCONUT, CUCUMBER, LIME, AND MINT COOLER

SERVES 4

INGREDIENTS

1 litre (2 pints) of coconut water

2 cucumbers, sliced very thinly
(save some for the garnish)

120 ml (4 fl oz) fresh lime juice
(about 4–5 limes)

50 g (2 oz) sugar (optional)

50 g (2 oz) mint leaves, chopped
(save some for the garnish)

METHOD

Combine the coconut water, cucumbers, lime juice, sugar and mint leaves in a large bowl. Stir so the ingredients are properly mixed through. Refrigerate for one to two hours.

Serve in tall glasses and garnish with some mint and cucumber slices.

BLUEBERRY MOJITO

SERVES 2

INGREDIENTS

Handful of fresh blueberries
50 ml (2 fl oz) fresh lime juice
(about 2 limes)
25 ml (1 fl oz) water
25 g (1 oz) sugar
Splash of sparkling water
6–8 mint leaves and a couple of
slices of lime, to garnish

METHOD

Add the sugar and water to a small saucepan. Heat gently, stirring all the time, until the sugar has dissolved. Allow to cool.

Crush the blueberries into a mushy consistency.

Add ice and all the ingredients except the mint leaves to a shaker.

Shake vigorously until blended.

Strain into two glasses and garnish with mint leaves and lime slices.

Sleep well

Improving your sleep will help you feel better and think more clearly. Sleep is the body's way of recharging itself, both physically and mentally. When you sleep better, life's difficulties and challenges can seem a little less stressful than they otherwise would.

Make your bedroom a sanctuary for sleep

Make your bedroom your sanctuary – a place for sleep and sex only. Leave your worries in another room and switch off while you prepare for sleep. One of the best ways to promote restful sleep is to declutter your surroundings. Keep your bedroom tidy, with clear floors, and find a home somewhere else in the house for everything that doesn't naturally belong there. Remove any tablets, phones, laptops and TVs – screen time should be limited before bedtime to prevent your brain "waking up" when it's really time to go to sleep. Read a book or a magazine instead. Opt for soft lighting to give the room a warm glow and try scented candles or oils to further create a relaxing and pleasant atmosphere. Lavender, chamomile, jasmine and vanilla are all believed to promote restful sleep.

CLEAR YOUR MIND BEFORE SLEEP

One of the most common causes of sleep loss is an overburdened mind. We've all experienced it – some more than others. It's important to learn to pack up your worries before you head to bed. You might find that writing down how you're feeling will help to unburden you – perhaps you could write in a diary or make a to-do list for the next day. You might also find that talking to a friend or family member helps to calm you; the aim is to feel as stress-free as possible before your head hits the pillow.

Sometimes the mind refuses to be quiet. In these cases, repeating a word which doesn't mean anything can help clear your mind of thoughts and, helpfully, induce boredom. One recommendation is to use the word "the", as this is short and means nothing on its own, though you can choose any word you think will work for you. Try repeating the word in your head every two seconds for five to ten minutes and let your mind be soothed into sleep.

GET ENOUGH SLEEP

Many of us lie awake at night worrying that we won't get the recommended eight hours of sleep that we need to function well. However, the "worry" part of this scenario is what has the biggest negative effect. Studies have shown that most people will have no problem functioning with six or seven hours of sleep, and, furthermore, that if you have lost sleep, you only need to catch up on about a third of the lost time to get back to normal. For example, if you went to bed an hour and a half late one night of the week, a 30-minute lie-in at the weekend would do the trick. Changing our perceptions of the time we need to sleep can help us to feel more secure and therefore help us sleep more easily, with a better quality of sleep.

Sleeping better

It is recommended that we have six to eight hours sleep per night. However, the reality is that most of us are having a lot less. Most of the time this is caused by stress, anxiety and a surplus of energy. Our lifestyles have become a lot more sedentary compared with our ancestors' and it's unnatural for our bodies to be sitting down all day. Try to be more active in your daily life, as exercising burns energy and will make you feel more tired in the evening. Complement the exercises in this book with walking up the stairs instead of using a lift or escalator, and taking a stroll to the local shop instead of driving. If you continue exercising, you'll notice the difference in your sleeping patterns and will feel fresher and revitalized.

BLUE LIGHT

The blue light from screens can disrupt melatonin production and increase cortisol. The rise of this stress hormone causes disturbed sleep, which increases risk of mental health problems, memory loss and depression. The brain also needs a minimum of five hours sleep a night to clean up toxins that have accumulated throughout the day and broken sleep hinders this process. It has also been suggested in a recent study carried out by the National Institute of Environmental Health Sciences in the USA that it's important to keep your phone a few feet away from your bed to avoid unnecessary low-level radiation, which can affect the functioning of your nervous system. Furthermore, new research from Brigham and Women's Hospital in Massachusetts concluded that reading from a screen before going to sleep has a significant impact on how alert you are the following day. If you struggle to keep off your smartphone, switch to "night shift" mode as this reduces blue-light emissions.

PART 3

FINDING
EQUILIBRIUM
AT HOME

Attaining and maintaining a happy and sustainable work–life balance is a tricky business these days, and if you feel that you've got it all wrong then you might have to think radically about how to change it. Although few of us are in a position to just stop working or easily find an alternative role, you can address the other areas of your life and get them in good shape to counter any imbalance. A great starting point is to make your home as comfortable as possible.

CREATE THE BEST ENVIRONMENT FOR YOU

Take time to think about what makes you feel at ease. It could be that you enjoy the simplicity of stripped back minimalism, with a neutral colour palette and no clutter. This sort of environment is a perfect setting to quieten your mind and help you to see clearly.

Alternatively, you might take comfort in a homely snug with lots of soft, tactile furnishings and blankets, rich colours and wall-to-wall bookshelves.

You'll be able to judge what suits you best, but if you're still unsure, there's plenty of inspiration to be found in interiors magazines or on social media sites such as Pinterest and Instagram. Spend a bit of time visualizing your perfect look – perhaps by creating a mood board – and then get started with a home makeover, one room at a time.

UPCYCLING IDEAS TO FRESHEN UP YOUR HOME

If it's change you're looking for, simply rearranging your furniture, adding a fresh coat of paint and putting up pictures can be cathartic. You don't always need to spend a fortune, either; there are some simple things you can do to brighten up existing furniture. The following pages will give you some ideas.

MAKE YOUR
HOME A HAVEN

Whatever your style, make sure your home is a haven, somewhere you feel safe and comfortable. The colour green symbolizes life, renewal, nature and energy, and is associated with harmony, freshness and safety. One of the easiest and cheapest ways to bring balance to your home is to invest in some potted plants. Not only do they look great, but they also absorb pollutants from the air, meaning you can breathe easy. Some scientists recommend having one plant for every 9 square metres (100 square feet) for the best purifying effects.

Light

Natural light is essential to our lives. It contributes to our happiness and well-being, it increases our alertness and improves mood and productivity. It also has a big impact on our body; it's how we make vitamin D, which is important for a healthy immune system and strong bones. There are numerous ways to introduce more natural light into the home; for example, swap heavy curtains for sheer panels – these could be lace or voile. Paint your walls in white, cream or soft grey to enhance the feeling of space, and position mirrors and furniture with glossy surfaces to reflect the light back into the room. Try some of these techniques and experience for yourself how a light, airy home creates a sense of peace and serenity.

Low-lighting

Think of emulating the cozy glow of an open fire — illuminate a room with one or two standard or desk lamps rather than an overhead light, which can be a little harsh.

CANDLELIGHT

Candles are not just great for creating the perfect ambience – scented candles can also bring harmony. Smells are strongly associated with emotion in our brains through the body's limbic system. You can use this to your advantage by filling your home with comforting aromas which instantly make you feel more relaxed. Candles scented with lavender or jasmine are calming, or if you want an energizing boost in the morning, try one with citrus notes.

BRINGING NATURE INTO THE HOME

Do you always come back from a walk with your pockets full of unusual stones, twigs and leaves? If you're stumped for what to do with your finds when you get back home, try making a nature display. It's great fun sorting through your findings and thinking of creative ways to display them. You could arrange a collection of shells and driftwood from the beach or place interesting rocks and pebbles in glass jars. Berry branches and pine cones look striking when arranged in large vases or they can be hung from the ceiling like a giant mobile. Don't limit your display to a table in the corner. Experiment by arranging your treasures in a tray or a box, or make a feature of them on a mantelpiece or shelf.

Declutter

Having a tidy home has a surprising impact on your general well-being; clear surfaces and a designated place for everything is calming, as you'll get to know where everything is and you won't have the stress of searching for those elusive objects like pens, paperclips and scissors. The act of tidying can be a soothing experience too. It offers a low-impact workout that produces serotonin, the mood-balancing hormone that makes us feel good. Many of us struggle with having too much stuff, and when it comes to decluttering it's tempting to put it off simply because, well, where do you start? Here are some tips on how to embrace decluttering, and even make it fun!

89

Clothes

Clothes are a weakness for many of us, but do you really know what you've got, and how much of it you actually wear? Begin by emptying and sorting one drawer at a time, or one cupboard at a time. For some items, deciding whether to let them go won't need much thought, but others can be tricky. This is when you should ask yourself the following questions:

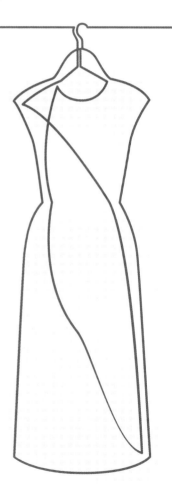

Do I love it?

Do I wear it?

Does it project the image I want to project?

Does it itch or scratch?

Can I actually move in it comfortably?

When did I last wear it?

Be honest, and soon you will have a large pile that can be sorted into categories: to be given away to friends and family, sold online, shwopped or taken to the charity shop.

SHWOPPING

This is a trendy word for clothes swapping, and is growing in popularity among the style-savvy and eco-conscious. It's a great example of sustainability, as it means that you can offload the clothes you don't wear or want in exchange for other people's preloved items, rather than heading to the shops to buy more. You could do this among your friends (why not host a shwopping party?) or sign up to the growing number of websites that offer this service.

Sustainable
shopping checklist

To reduce clutter, think before you buy. The next time you see something you want to buy, ask yourself the following questions:

Can I live without it?

Will I wear it or use it?
If so, where and when?

Can I afford it?

Would I prefer to have the money in my account or this item in my house?

Have I got the space for it?

If you're still not sure, the best thing to do is sleep on it, then go back and buy it the next day if you're convinced you must have it. Alternatively, have a rule that if you buy something you must get rid of something, so you're never adding to your amount of belongings.

Paperwork and correspondence

It's amazing how quickly receipts fill your purse and household documents multiply into paper monoliths on your desk or kitchen surface. How much of it do you really need? This little guide should help reduce your paper use.

Warranties and user guides – throw away anything pertaining to something that you no longer need or use, and any warranties that are no longer in date. Most user guides can be accessed online, but keep ones for new-ish products.

Magazines and newspapers – cancel subscriptions for magazines that you don't read and subscribe to online newsagents instead, where you pay a monthly fee for unlimited access to all the latest magazines. Most newspapers offer an online-only subscription too. Proudly display the magazines that you are keeping in a rack or in a small(ish) pile on the coffee table, and recycle the ones you don't want or take them to the local doctor's surgery for their waiting room.

Bills – pay them and then file them, but throw away after a couple of years.

Bank statements – go paperless and check your statements online.

Receipts – keep receipts for big-ticket items but discard everyday receipts after a month. Many shops and businesses offer to send receipts electronically via email, so opt for this as an alternative.

Insurance documents – keep the valid ones only.

Work/tax documents – keep payslips and tax-related documents for two years from the end of the tax year that they relate to. If self-employed, hold on to these documents for six years from the end of the tax year that they relate to. Store any documents you need to keep in a labelled and dated concertina file, and the next time you receive something you want to keep safe, pop it in straight away!

Books

Go through your books and decide which
ones truly deserve a place on your bookshelf
and in your life — the ones that moved
you, the ones that are too beautiful to
part with, the ones that were gifted with
inscriptions, the ones autographed by your
favourite writer — then be honest about
the ones that you are never going to read
or refer to again. Take these to a charity
shop, ready to be loved by someone else.

GET OUT INTO THE GARDEN

Being outside and at one with nature has proven health benefits, so if you are lucky enough to have a garden, make the most of it. Keeping on top of gardening can be a proper workout and the exertion required in activities such as lawn mowing, hedge trimming, digging, raking or sweeping all have an aerobic effect which releases endorphins, the stress-relieving hormones. Gardening involves many critical functions beyond the obvious physical ones such as strength and dexterity; for instance the problem-solving, learning and sensory stimulation have been shown to alleviate mental health symptoms such as depression and low self-esteem. One more tangential benefit is a boost to immunity – half-moons of mud in your fingernails is good for you because the bacteria in common garden soil has been found to ease asthma and skin conditions such as psoriasis.

Jam jar herbs

If you don't have a garden you can still reap the benefits of home-grown produce by creating some herb planters. These are not only decorative but they're a neat way of growing your own herbs on your kitchen windowsill.

YOU WILL NEED

Young herb plants, such as parsley, thyme, basil, oregano, coriander, rosemary, mint or chive (you can purchase these from supermarkets or garden centres)
A selection of jam jars
Potting compost
Soil cover stones
Water

METHOD

Clean your jam jars with washing-up liquid and warm water, then rinse and leave to dry.

Fill the base of your jars with stones – make sure it's a minimum of 3 cm (1.2 in.) in depth. These stones are vital as they will draw the water and prevent mould forming on your plants. Add a good handful of potting soil to each jar, leaving enough room to add your plants.

Remove the baby herb plants from their containers and gently tap the roots with your fingers to loosen the soil around it. Then plant the herbs in the jars – one per jar.

Add more potting soil to the top and pat it down around the base of each plant.

Water your plants and then place on a windowsill, making sure they're not in direct sunlight.

Now you can enjoy herbs all year round, and they're easy to grab when you're preparing meals.

DRYING HERBS FOR YEAR-ROUND USE

Sturdy herbs, such as dill, bay, rosemary and oregano, can be air-dried on a windowsill. Moisture-rich herbs, such as basil, lemon balm and mint, are best dried in the oven at super-low temperatures as this speeds up the process and avoids mould.

Before air-drying herbs, cut and remove any dry or diseased leaves. Shake gently to remove any insects or rinse with cool water and pat completely dry with paper towels (wet herbs will moulder and rot). Remove the lower leaves along the bottom couple of centimetres or so of each branch. Bundle four to six branches together and tie as a bunch using string or a rubber band, then leave these on a windowsill or a sunny spot in the house. You can even hang them on a makeshift washing line and use pegs to keep them in place. The bundles will shrink as they dry and the rubber band will loosen, so check periodically that they are not slipping.

Another method for drying sturdier herbs such as rosemary is to make small bundles, tying the bunches together with string or a rubber band as before. Punch or cut several holes in a paper bag. Label the bag with the name of the herb to be dried and place the herb bundle upside down in the bag. Gather the ends of the bag around the bundle and tie closed. Make sure the herbs are not crowded inside the bag. Hang the bag upside down in a warm, airy room and leave for at least two weeks. Keep checking weekly until the herbs are dry and ready to store.

Once dried, store your herbs in airtight containers in a cool, dark place. They should remain fresh for up to two years.

THE HEALING POWER OF HERBS

Basil – this luscious annual plant with spoon-shaped leaves is a medicinal herb, which adds wonderful flavour to pizzas, pastas and salads. It has antidepressant qualities and boosts the immune system.

Lavender – just the heady scent of this purple-blue flower is therapeutic, but when made into a balm or salve its antiseptic qualities can help to heal cuts and wounds.

Rosemary – this spikey and woody medicinal herb helps memory and concentration as well as sweetening bad breath. Make your own cold cure by gathering fresh rosemary from the garden, plunging it into a bowl of boiling water and then carefully inhaling the vapours from the infusion.

Peppermint – this potent herb can be taken in an infusion to relieve indigestion. It also helps to reduce nausea and headaches with its stress-relieving and anti-inflammatory qualities.

Parsley – this pretty, deep-green plant comes in both flat and curly leafed varieties. It's often used as a garnish but, chopped finely, it's a great accompaniment to many sauces. It's packed full of nutrients and has healing powers to help ease stomach acid and bad breath. Just pick a few fresh leaves and chew!

Sage – Sage's genus name, *Salvia*, means "to heal", reflecting its early use as a medicinal, not culinary, herb. It can help provide relief for mouth and throat inflammations. Sage leaves can also be brewed into a tea for gargling as an antiseptic. If you have toothache, grind a handful of dried sage leaves with a dessertspoon of table salt with a pestle and mortar, then mix with a little water so it forms a paste, then swish in your mouth for a couple of minutes before spitting it out.

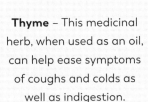

Thyme – This medicinal herb, when used as an oil, can help ease symptoms of coughs and colds as well as indigestion.

Lemon balm – a relative of mint, lemon balm is a versatile medicinal herb that helps relieve anxiety, insomnia, wounds, insect bites and an upset stomach. It also speeds the healing of cold sores.

Chamomile – the flower heads of this daisy-like plant have multiple uses. When dried and made into an infusion, they can soothe indigestion as well as calm a worried mind. Creams can be made with chamomile to ease skin inflammations and irritations. In the same way that chamomile is used to soothe a person who is out of sorts, it can also be used to give an ailing plant a lift when it is planted beside it.

PART 4

SPEND
QUALITY TIME
WITH OTHERS

Our busy lives can sometimes make us forget what is truly important and we neglect the simple things that actually bring us joy and pleasure. We are naturally social creatures, and socializing should be a key part of our lives. Imagine if you were made to stay alone with no interaction with people: most of us would struggle with the loneliness. However, as we grow more and more dependent on technology we seem to spend an increasing amount of time isolating ourselves in a virtual world. It's time to redress the balance.

Get off your gadgets

Too much time on a tablet or watching TV and too little movement is unhealthy. The average adult spends around ten hours per day looking at a screen. The way to get active and away from screens is to install a few healthy practices, such as:

Needless to say, phones and tablets should be a no-no at the table!

Rather than going cold turkey, ease yourself into reducing screen time by an hour at first, and gradually increase this time. You're more likely to stick to your new regime and less likely to rebound back into old habits.

Keep track of screen time to get a clear picture of how much time you spend on your gadgets – use an app or simply switch off the Wi-Fi connection after an hour or two, and make sure the time is well spent. Try doing something else that you enjoy such as reading, listening to music or catching up with friends, rather than scrolling endlessly through Instagram or Facebook.

Try to eat with a companion or companions – we all have to eat and it's the best reason to sit down together and nurture friendships and relationships. Ask direct questions to get the conversation flowing, such as "How was your meeting with X?" or "What was the best part of your day?" See "Eat together" on p.106.

Be mindful of media consumption and what you absorb. For example, think about how scrolling through news websites before you go to bed might affect you. Limit your worries and allow yourself to enjoy your last hour before bed by reading a good book or having a conversation with your partner, or calling up a friend and having a good conversation.

Book in time with a friend or loved one. It could be as simple as going to the park or swimming – anything that will engage you for up to an hour. You'll find that these pockets of time will become special and enjoyable.

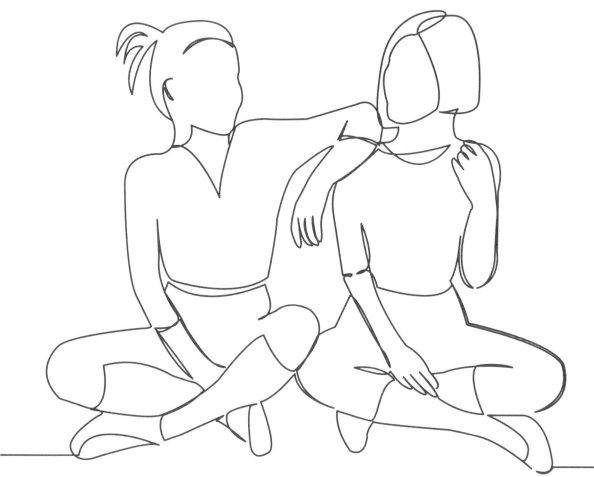

Your opinions matter, whatever your point of view might be. Regardless of your views, you will never make an impact unless you share your thoughts and ideas. When we collaborate and exchange them, we learn more about ourselves and are then able to apply that knowledge in making better decisions.

Feel good speaking aloud

Having the confidence to share your feelings and opinions with people is easier said than done. Some people are naturals, while others shy away or tend to agree with the people they are speaking to, even if they disagree.

To help you find your voice, try practising mantras every day to help build your self-esteem. Mantras are positive words or phrases that you repeat to yourself, either out loud or in your head, and they help stop negative trains of thought. If you find yourself regularly thinking "I shouldn't say that in case I embarrass myself", your mantra could be as simple as "I have a valid point and it should be shared". Say this to yourself in a mirror at home or in your head before you want to express your thoughts to someone. You'll be surprised by how much other people appreciate your ideas.

Eat together

Make a point of eating with someone on a regular basis. Be it with a friend, room-mate, partner or family member. Many of us scarf down a sandwich at lunchtime while browsing the internet, or eat separately from those we live with because everyone has different plans for the evening and at weekends. A recent report discovered that the average family eats together only once every five days. Sitting around a table and sharing a meal is a simple way to reconnect with each other, to share news, views and ideas, and to check in with how everyone is doing.

Picnics

Make your mealtime into an occasion by organizing a picnic outdoors. Head to a beautiful and restful setting, such as a beach, park, forest or nature reserve, and spread out some blankets to sit on. Ask everyone to bring a dish and let everyone help themselves. Keep things simple with a homemade quiche and salad, or something warming like hot soup, chilli or stew in a flask, baked potatoes wrapped in foil, and hot chocolate and cookies for dessert. Food always tastes better outside.

Potluck meals

Host a potluck meal at your home once a month. Send out messages on social media inviting your favourite people over – don't say it's compulsory but ask for an RSVP so you know how many mouths there are to feed, then each person attending can bring part of the meal, whether it's drinks, starters, mains, etc. If you're feeling confident – and have the space – invite each person to bring a plus one. It's a great way to expand your social circle and try new dishes.

PLAY
TOGETHER

Search your attic – or your parents' – and dig out some of your favourite board games. Playing games is a great way to connect with the people in your life and focus on having fun. Play a classic game such as Scrabble, Ludo, Backgammon, Monopoly or Cluedo, or test your physical and mental dexterity with Jenga. If you don't have any board games, try some of these old-fashioned games with friends and family.

THE STRANGEST STORY

PLAYERS

Four or more.

WHAT YOU WILL NEED

Some paper and a pen each.

HOW TO PLAY

Players should take a sheet of paper and write a silly or strange sentence on it: for example: "The giraffe sunbathed with Santa Claus" or "Elvis thought the moon was made of cheese." The paper should then be passed left so the next player can illustrate it. The original sentence should then be folded over and the paper passed left so the next player can write down an interpretation of the drawing. The drawing should then be folded over so the next player can illustrate the new sentence, and so on until you have run out of paper. Now for the best bit: unfold the paper and share the full story.

TWENTY QUESTIONS

HOW TO PLAY

Choose a player to start. This player should think of an object – anything from a potato to Bart Simpson's skateboard, a monster truck or a walnut – and tell the other players whether it is animal, vegetable or mineral. The other players must then ask questions with yes or no answers and guess the correct object before they hit twenty questions. Whoever successfully guesses the object becomes the next player to pick an item and answer the questions.

PLAYERS

Four or more.

WHAT YOU WILL NEED

A sharp mind and quick responses.

CAPTURE THE FLAG

PLAYERS

Eight or more.

WHAT YOU WILL NEED

A park or large garden, two flags (or tea towels).

HOW TO PLAY

This one works best with lots of players and a decent-sized garden or area of a park. Players are split into two teams and each team has five minutes to hide their flag on their designated half of the playing area. Each team should also choose a base area. You should be able to see a bit of the flag poking out from its hiding place and it should be easy enough to grab, so don't bury it or tie it to anything.

Players should try their hardest to get hold of the other team's flag – by hiding behind trees, crawling on their hands and knees and generally being swift as anything – and bring it back to their base without being tagged by a member of the other team. If you do get caught, you get put in "prison" (a designated patch of grass) but can be freed at the touch of one of your team members. Whoever gets back to base first with the other team's flag wins.

MAKE
TIME
TO
CALL

It's easy for time to slip **away** from you and to forget to keep up with the really important people in your life, especially the ones that live far **away** who you don't get to see much. Don't neglect loved ones **and** friends, **and** make an effort to schedule some time on **a** weekly basis to pick up the phone and speak with someone rather than messaging them.

PĀRT 5

GET BACK TO NATURE IN YOUR DOWN TIME

There are numerous studies on the health benefits of being out in the open air, from lowering blood pressure and stress levels, to providing a natural mood-boost from the ions in plants, trees and bodies of water. There are also the obvious benefits to physical health if you engage in outdoor activities, and spending time outside can foster a greater appreciation of our natural environment. This section offers ways to reconnect with nature and make the most of your time in the great outdoors.

FOREST
THERAPY

The forest is a therapeutic landscape, one that can be enjoyed without the need to accomplish anything.

Listening to the sound of the trees rustling and swaying, the satisfying crunch of autumn leaves underfoot, the call of a cuckoo – there are many simple pleasures to be enjoyed when spending time in the woods. The Japanese have a special term for it, forest bathing, which means being in the presence of trees. Forest bathing became part of the public health programme in Japan in the 1980s as research proved that it has numerous benefits: it lowers heart rate and blood pressure, reduces stress hormone production, boosts the immune system and improves overall feelings of well-being.

THE GREAT OUTDOORS

To be surrounded by nature uninterrupted as far as the eye can see is a rare and wonderful thing. There are still such wild and beautiful places – ones that are off the beaten track and involve scrambling through hedges or wading through streams or marshes. Unfold a paper map and look for open moorland, chalk valleys, marshes, large areas of woodland or coastal paths and set a course for adventure.

Escape

We often create routines in our lives that are difficult to break away from. Make sure you balance your life with spontaneous days out, no matter how small, to awaken your senses and help you remember what your priorities are. Here are some ideas to get you going.

Take a train to the coast

Pack your swimming things (plus a sweater in case of a chilly sea breeze) and a picnic for a day at the beach. Let the adventure begin once you step on the train, making sure your seat is on the seaward side. Travelling by train affords sweeping views and a chance to slow down and switch off. Let your mind wander as you watch the world go by in a blur of greens, blues and golds, or settle into a good book, but keep an eye out for that first glimmer of the sea on the horizon.

Once you arrive at your destination, there's no need to fight with the traffic or circle around for a parking space. Simply make your way to the shore. Look out for hedgerows on the way – blackberries growing close to the ocean are infused with a salty tang.

Find the perfect spot for a day of watching the world go by and absorbing vitamin D. Experience the positive effects of being close to water – the minerals and negative ions in the sea air improve the flow of oxygen to the brain and boost serotonin levels, producing a meditative effect. If you're feeling brave, take to the waters for some wild swimming (see p.132).

WALK OR CLIMB TO A HIGH POINT AND WATCH THE SUNRISE

Pick a dry morning and put on your walking boots and coat – it's often cold before sunrise even in the summer months, and the ground may be wet with dew. Set out to the highest point in your locale, such as a hill or a cliff. Make sure it's safe and accessible at this time of day, take a phone and torch with you, and let someone know where you will be. Better still, take a companion.

As well as a chance to view the sunrise, going for a walk before the rest of the world wakes can lead to some exciting opportunities to see nocturnal animals. Be slow and silent and respect the natural habitat that you are walking through. Listen out for the rustling of wildlife, such as badgers and birds, as they scavenge for insects and seeds. Look up as the stars begin to fade. Find a spot to sit and watch the sunrise. Try to clear your mind and simply soak up the sunlight and listen to the hum of the world as it wakes.

EXPLORE LOCAL HISTORY

There are places steeped in history on almost everyone's doorstep, whether it's rock formations or standing stones, earthworks, an ancient yew forest or a castle ruin. Seek these out, soak up the atmosphere, take photos and feel connected to the past; imagine what it would have been like there perhaps a century or several millennia ago.

GET LOST!

You don't need to plan any elaborate excursions to discover and experience something new. Try this simple idea for size.

Take a walk with at least one other person and from your front door take it in turns to say "left" or "right" so that each time you approach a left-hand or right-hand turn, you take the suggested direction. You'll go on a walk that you've possibly never been on before.

See the world from a different perspective

If you're looking for the thrill of adventure, reach for new heights and try tree climbing.

Find a tree with sturdy, low-hanging branches, and clamber over and around them, noticing the new perspectives you get even from being just a few extra feet off the ground. Or, if you want more of a challenge, you could try recreational tree climbing. Companies that offer this will be able to provide you with safety gear and ropes which allow you to scale the tallest trees – you will feel your spirit soar as you survey the forest from high above.

Climbing a tree is the perfect way to embrace what the woods have to offer and this great year-round activity has the added benefit of improving your muscle strength and giving you a sense of accomplishment too.

Note: Do not climb trees on your own. Always ensure that the tree is safe to climb and can hold your weight. Never climb higher that you can safely get down from.

GO ON AN ADVENTURE

The feeling of doing something that is greater and more exciting than your usual weekly tasks will help you feel more alive, as the adrenaline starts coursing through your body. Try one of the following activities and enjoy the magic it brings.

ORIENTEERING

Orienteering is the perfect activity for those who like to get competitive. The purpose of this adventure sport is to get from A to B as quickly as possible, with the help of a map and a compass. Dress appropriately and wear sturdy shoes as you're likely to be tackling several tricky terrains.

TAKE A HIKE

Hiking – or walking – is one of the easiest ways to get out into the fresh air and to make the most of the great outdoors. As well as being a good cardiovascular workout and an opportunity to see nature at your own pace, it's also excellent for brain health. The hippocampus, the part of that brain which consolidates short- and long-term memory, uses sight, sound and smells to create mental maps; going for a hike is one of the best ways to supply this part of the brain with new sensory stimuli.

Be prepared for all types of terrain by investing in a pair of sturdy walking boots. Check the weather and dress accordingly, packing essentials such as water, snacks, sunscreen, a map and a phone.

LOOK AT THE STARS

A clear night is the perfect time to explore the wonders of the night sky. All you need is a star map and some binoculars in order to spot some stunning celestial objects. Download an evening sky map from the internet and buy or borrow a compass to help you navigate the night sky. It's best to stargaze away from cities and areas with light pollution – try a park, a hill or a beach. Seek out the North Star and constellations such as the Plough, Orion and Cassiopeia. Look out for planets and shooting stars, too. Make sure you dress warmly and take a blanket to lie on.

Go wild

Sometimes you just need to get away from it all — somewhere the Wi-Fi won't reach and you can't be disturbed by someone showing off on Facebook. The answer is to go wild!

Wild camping

Camping is one of the most accessible ways to take a break from the everyday and spend time outdoors. If you're feeling adventurous, try camping in the woods or in a farmer's field, but always seek permission from the landowner and do a recce first to assess whether it's a safe place to spend the night. There are a number of factors when considering a place to make camp:

- Never pitch up at the bottom of a hill or slope – it might feel sheltered there but if it rains you'll soon know about it when your tent and the ground around it becomes waterlogged. Instead, choose somewhere level which has slightly soft ground.

- Make sure there are no hazards above you, such as power lines or trees, because if there are high winds, these could cost you your life.

- Pitch up so that the back of your tent is facing into the wind for maximum protection from the elements.

- Even if you love being near water, don't camp closer than 100 metres (328 feet) to the water – 200 metres (656 feet) away is preferable. This is in line with wild camping's main rule of "leave no trace" and ensures the preservation of the ecosystem that the water supports.

Making a campfire

There are few things more bonding and calming than sitting round a campfire with companions or loved ones, and watching the flames dance and hearing them crackle. Building a campfire is easy to do once you've mastered the basics.

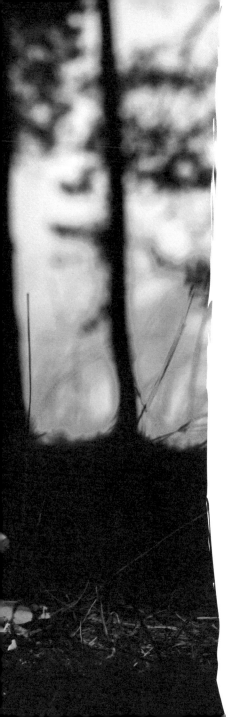

- Find a safe area which is away from fences, trees, bushes, buildings and any household rubbish or garden waste.

- Dig a shallow pit to contain the fire. It should be approximately 10 cm (4 in.) deep and about a metre (3 feet) wider than you'd like your fire to be.

- Place bricks or large stones around the edge of the pit to contain the fire.

- Put some fire lighters in the centre of the pit and add a bundle of tinder on top (you can use wood shavings, newspaper, twigs, bark, grass, dry leaves and even moss).

- Arrange dry kindling over the tinder at 45-degree angles, meeting in the middle to form the shape of a tepee. Leave some gaps in the kindling so the oxygen can reach the tinder.

- Place a lit match under your tinder or drop it inside the tepee. The tinder should catch light, followed by the kindling.

- When the kindling tepee collapses, add logs to fuel the fire.

- At the end of the evening, make sure you put the fire out completely. This takes longer than you think – leave at least 20 minutes for this. Sprinkle water over the fire to put out the embers and, when cool, pile some dirt or sand on top.

- Don't allow children near the fire without adult supervision.

A FORAGING WALK IN THE WOODS

Foraging is a great way to reconnect with nature while enjoying the outdoors, and hedgerows and woodlands burst with delicious edible treasure; fruits such as sloes, blackberries and elderberries are just asking to be picked. The next time you are out walking, take a basket and harvest the wild hedgerows. Pluck blackberries from bushes to make a fruit crumble, pick bunches of ripe elderberries for a delicious sweet jelly, or collect the flowers to make cordial. Make sure you take a guidebook or expert with you so you know what's safe to eat, and *never* eat anything you're unsure of. Look out for wild garlic on the forest floor in the spring before it flowers. Let your nose guide you, as you will soon discover this plant has a heady aroma. The leaves are somewhat similar to lily of the valley, which is poisonous, so just be sure you have picked the correct leaves: crush the leaves between your fingers for that distinctive garlic smell. For mushrooms and fungi, always make sure you consult an expert before picking with a view to eating, as some can be highly poisonous.

Wild garlic soup

This simple soup is great for sharing, and tastes even better when you have sourced the fresh wild garlic on a walk beforehand.

SERVES 4

PREPARATION TIME: 20 minutes
COOKING TIME: 25 minutes

INGREDIENTS

25 g (1 oz) butter
2 potatoes, diced
1 onion, chopped
1 litre (2 pts) chicken or vegetable stock
2 large handfuls of wild garlic leaves, washed and roughly chopped
110 ml (4 fl oz) single cream
Crusty bread and grated parmesan cheese, to serve

METHOD

Over a medium heat, melt the butter in a large saucepan. When it's foaming, add the potatoes and onion, and toss in the butter until well coated, then season with salt and pepper. Turn the heat down, cover the pan and cook for ten minutes or until vegetables are soft, stirring regularly so that the vegetables don't stick and burn.

Next, add stock and bring to a rolling boil, then add the wild garlic leaves and cook for two minutes or until the leaves have wilted. Don't overcook or it will lose its fresh green colour and flavour.

Pour into a blender and blitz until smooth, return to the pan, stir in the cream and season to taste. Serve hot with crusty bread and grated parmesan cheese.

ELDERFLOWER CORDIAL

A refreshing summer drink that'll taste even better than store-bought stuff as you foraged the elderflower yourself.

MAKES approx. 1 litre (2 pints)

PREPARATION TIME

10 minutes

COOKING TIME

12 hours (or overnight)

INGREDIENTS

20 elderflower heads
1 litre (2 pts) water
650 g (1.5 lb)
caster sugar
Zest and juice of
2 unwaxed lemons
Zest and juice of
1 unwaxed lime

METHOD

Give the flower heads a good shake to rid them of any insects, then rinse thoroughly.

In a large pan, bring the water to a simmer before adding the sugar. Once the sugar has dissolved, remove from the heat, add the zest and juice of the lemons and lime, and stir.

Add the elderflower heads to the pan, making sure that the flowers are submerged. Then slice the remaining lemon rind and add it to the pan as well.

Cover and leave to infuse overnight.

Strain the liquid through muslin or a clean cotton tea towel. Pour into bottles with screw-top lids. The cordial will keep for up to three weeks in the fridge.

Serve diluted with tonic water or added to drinks such as prosecco, white wine or gin.

WILD SWIMMING

Wild swimming is simply swimming outdoors and it is everything you enjoy about your local pool but with a difference.

Wild swimming is much more than swimming lengths. It's about reconnecting with nature, and getting the most out of being in the open. It's a full-body experience of the world around you; it involves all of your senses, and no two swims are ever the same.

There are many health benefits to swimming, all of which are enhanced by venturing out into the open air rather than swimming indoors. Not only does it improve your fitness in a sustainable way, as it's a non-impact sport, but the cold water invigorates you, and embracing the chill can even be the source of a natural high. Swimming outdoors and engaging with the world around you as you swim has also been shown to improve your mood and alleviate feelings of depression.

Another benefit is that it's a low-cost activity. This simple, wholesome pleasure is open to anyone and everyone. And, if it becomes something you love, it could take you all over the world in search of ever more beautiful scenery to swim in.

WILD SWIMMING TOP TIPS

If you're worried about the cold, invest in a wetsuit or wetsuit boots and gloves, and a swimming cap to keep your extremities warmer.

Never jump into the water if you don't know how deep it is, as this could cause serious injury. If it is safe to jump, acclimatize your body to the water temperature by paddling or dangling your feet in first to prevent your body from going into shock.

Know your ability: it sounds obvious, but before you embark on a wild swimming adventure, make sure that you are proficient at swimming. If you're unsure, ask a lifeguard at your local pool for advice, and the first time you swim in the open make sure you take it slowly. You don't have to push yourself to enjoy the benefits of the water.

Always swim with a buddy if you can, or at the very least make sure that someone knows where you're going and when you expect to return. Alternatively, notify someone on the shore that you're going out so they can watch out for you.

Cover any cuts before you get in, try not to swallow any water, and shower thoroughly once you're done swimming. It's very unlikely that you will catch an illness from wild swimming, but minimizing the risk is always best practice.

Always swim around the edge of the lake rather than across the middle. This way, if there is a problem you'll be closer to help.

Always do your research before you swim. Are the any regulations to follow? Is it private property? Are there any tides or currents to be aware of? Are there any rocky areas to watch out for? Where is it safe to enter and leave the lake?

PART 6

NEVER STOP LEARNING

People have sought self-improvement and enlightenment throughout the ages, and with good reason. Setting yourself goals and challenges, whether work-related or for your own development, such as learning a new skill or sport, can help you to switch off from the high pressures of daily life. By continuing to learn and further your understanding of yourself and what makes you tick, you become more emotionally resilient and better able to deal with life's ups and downs.

LEARN FROM THE PAST BUT LIVE IN THE PRESENT

Often when we are in the middle of a difficult situation, it can be hard to see a comfortable way to resolve it without becoming stressed. Here's how to pause and consider the problem in a more mindful way. When faced with a tricky situation, many of us catastrophize, imagining the worst possible outcome. Instead of allowing your mind to unravel, bring yourself back to the present. A large proportion of things we imagine never actually happen. Remind yourself that you are not a fortune teller. Worrying serves no purpose other than to make you feel anxious. Focus on the facts of a situation and on what is, rather than the "what-ifs".

SELF-COMPASSION

Another important skill to learn to become more resilient in tough situations is to adopt self-compassion. The ability to forgive yourself during difficult times is crucial. Self-compassion will enable you to pick yourself up, dust yourself off and try again. If you beat yourself up every time you falter, you will be far less likely to succeed in your goals, which will impact on your confidence and, in turn, your health and happiness.

Discover new things

Take the time to ask yourself how often you try something new. We often follow the same routine day after day, rarely thinking about the processes or indeed questioning why we're doing things the same way each time. Trying new things is important for brain health as well as reinvigorating your life with a fresh perspective.

Say "yes" to the road less travelled

It's easy and comfortable to retreat from new experiences. Our natural default is often one of fear of the unknown, but once you retrain your mind to say yes to new things, the fear will slowly dissolve and you will begin to see new challenges as an opportunity to bring energy and excitement into your life. The other benefit to saying yes is that it helps to expand self-knowledge – perhaps it turns out that you have a natural aptitude for learning a new language or dance style – which in turn leads to greater contentment as you learn more about who you are and what makes you tick. When you are trying something new, you stimulate your creative mind which positively affects all areas of your life, as it enables you to express yourself in new ways.

Develop new skills

As well as stimulating the brain, learning new skills helps to distract you from the 101 chores that you need to do. You'll also feel a sense of accomplishment as you teach yourself skills you never thought you could learn.

BRAIN EXERCISES

Often called brain training, the practice of exposing your brain to new experiences that stimulate your senses and trigger emotional responses can dramatically improve memory and lessen the effects of ageing on your grey cells. Here are some fun ways to get your brain working differently and more effectively.

SHAKE-UP YOUR DAILY ROUTINE

Begin by brushing your teeth with your non-dominant hand. Feed your pets before you make breakfast – or vice-versa if you usually do it this way round. Take in a podcast or listen to a different radio station on your way to work, or walk a different route. Change your view at your desk – replace your desktop picture, move around the objects on your desk or even move your desk altogether so that you can relate differently to the people and objects around you. Really notice these differences and try to experience them fully. Mixing things up will increase brain activity and give you a boost.

FOLLOW YOUR NOSE

Smells can make you travel in time. A smell can unearth long-forgotten memories: the scent of vanilla ice cream could evoke the memory of it dripping on your hands as a small child or freshly cut grass could be associated with school sports day. Linking a new smell to an action can stimulate new pathways in the brain. Try smelling an essential oil or flower when you come home of an evening, until you associate it with being home.

CREATE SOMETHING BEAUTIFUL

Painting and drawing, or any kind of artistic enterprise, activates the parts of the brain that process colours, forms and textures. Give this part of your brain a workout by writing a list of random words and then doodling an image of what each word makes you think of – it needn't be literal; the more abstract the better.

KEEP YOUR MIND ACTIVE

Do a
Zumba
workout.

There are infinite ways to keep your mind
active. Here are a few ideas to try:

Do some
gardening.

Volunteer
for a
charity.

Plan and
host a soirée.

Try a
circus skills
workshop.

**Write a
song, just for
yourself.**

Write
letters to
your friends
and family.

Do
some
DIY.

Learn a
new word
every day.

Do a
crossword
puzzle.

**Read
a book.**

Write a diary.

Learn how to knit.

Play a board game.

Sit in silence for five minutes and write down every noise you can hear.

Make thumb-pots out of clay.

Learn a language.

Bake a cake with your favourite flavours.

Hire a tandem bike and go for a ride with your favourite person.

Count the number of species of animals and birds you see and hear on a walk.

Invent a signature dish or drink.

Learn to play a musical instrument.

Go to a dance class.

PART 7

BE PART OF SOMETHING BIGGER

As humans we need a sense of belonging, and it's the ways you interact with the wider community that can enhance your well-being. The benefits of being part of a group are endless, from having a natural support network to being inspired by others. For instance, rather than having to learn from your own mistakes or successes, you can reach out to the community and ask if anyone has had an experience that could be valuable to your situation. Broaden your mind and see things from a new perspective when you mix with people from outside your natural friendship group and find a new balance to your life.

GIVING BACK TO THE COMMUNITY

Hold a cake sale for charity

Consider either holding a cake sale at your workplace or hosting a coffee morning at your home and dedicating the proceeds to a local charity.

Help out at a community garden

A community garden is a patch of land where you can exercise your green fingers and learn a few tips along the way, as well as meeting people with similar interests. Go to communitygarden.org or farmgarden.org.uk for more information.

Help the homeless

Offer to help at a refuge for the homeless by making and serving meals, or by donating blankets and warm clothes such as coats, woollen socks and sturdy shoes.

Become a sponsor

If you have a particular interest and want to make a regular donation, look up ways to donate to a preferred charity or how to become a sponsor. You could help a female survivor of war by sponsoring her to learn skills to support her family, or sponsor a child refugee to ensure they have adequate food and shelter via savethechildren.org.

Offering your time is a wonderful way to engage with your community and share your skills and energy. Here are some ways to give back close to home.

Coach a youth sports team

There are openings in almost every sport in every community for compassionate teachers and volunteer coaches. This is a way of inspiring and motivating children to enjoy sports and will keep you physically active too. You don't always have to have experience or qualifications, especially if you are the assistant.

Speak up

Your voice counts. If you have a particular concern relating to your community, write to and lobby the governing body where you live and urge them to act. Set up online petitions via websites such as change.org for issues that you feel strongly about. If you have been the victim of sexism, speak out on everydaysexism.com. Frequent small steps can lead to big changes.

Volunteer at your local school

Children need role models and people who care about their lives and behaviour. Whether you read stories to younger school children, monitor outdoor activities, help out on field trips or spend a Saturday tidying and litter-picking on the school grounds, your efforts will be recognized and appreciated.

Combat loneliness

Help to combat the loneliness epidemic and volunteer to spend time with an older, isolated person in your community. You may have a neighbour who doesn't have many visitors, or their family might live too far away to be a regular part of their lives. Offer to do small things for them, like tidying their garden or doing some grocery shopping, and don't underestimate the value of just stopping by for a chat.

Simple acts of kindness

It's the little things that can mean the most, from giving a loved one a call to surprising a friend with a bunch of flowers, and the best part is that doing good things makes you feel good too! Here's a list of small but important acts of kindness to weave into your everyday life.

Be a good listener.

Offer your seat to someone on the bus or train.

Tell someone when they've done something well.

Loan someone a book or DVD that you think they would like.

Bring your loved ones a drink in bed in the morning.

Offer a colleague a lift to work.

Phone a relative or old friend for a good chat.

Bring healthy treats to work for your colleagues – no more cake!

Give someone a compliment: it will make their day.

Pick up litter instead of walking past it. People will notice, and hopefully follow suit.

Hold the door open for the next person.

Be patient.

Give away flowers or vegetables from your garden or make some cakes for a new neighbour, or even an old neighbour!

Remind your loved ones how much you love them.

Write a letter – it is so much nicer to receive a letter via traditional post instead of email.

Remember your friends' birthdays – send them a card or take them out for a drink.

Offer encouragement to someone who is feeling low.

Put out your neighbours' bins on bin day.

BE GRATEFUL FOR WHAT YOU HAVE

Start a daily gratitude journal. List all the positive things in your life — from the small things that make you smile, such as the view from your window, to the bigger things, like your health or your family. At night, list three things you were grateful for during the day. You'll soon start focusing naturally on the positives.

THINKING ABOUT THE FUTURE

Living a more balanced life invites you to consider the needs of the environment as well as those of your local community and beyond. There are a variety of ways that you can do your bit, and this section offers all manner of ideas to get you inspired. Just think how different the world would be if we all made one positive change.

LOOK AFTER THE ENVIRONMENT

Leave the car at home

The next time you need to go somewhere that's less than a couple of miles away, stop yourself from getting in the car and walk or ride your bike there instead. Not only will you not be contributing to harmful carbon emissions by leaving the car at home, but you're also getting exercise and you're more than likely to bump into people you know, so the social aspect is a possible benefit too.

Take a staycation

Make a promise to holiday closer to home instead of taking a flight. Not only will you significantly reduce your carbon footprint, but you are also likely to save money.

Think before you take-away

Coffee will always be popular, but those paper cups that you have for your takeaway coffee end up in landfill. According to the UK's Friends of the Earth, around 2.5 billion of them end in landfill and only one in 400 is recycled. That's a lot of cups. Do your bit by taking a reusable cup and asking the barista to fill it instead of using a disposable one. Some coffee shops will give you a discount for doing this, but the fact that you're not adding to landfill is enough of a reward, right?

Go paperless

We all receive a lot of mail, but how much of it do we really need? There are simple ways to reduce paper post, such as paying bills online, subscribing to online bank statements and unsubscribing from catalogues. Borrow books and read magazines from a library – the best part is that it's free!

Use less plastic

We've all been educated about the effects of plastic on wildlife, especially marine animals.* Here are some simple tips to eliminate or at least reduce your plastic use:

Buy a reusable flask to fill with water from the tap; if you have takeaway coffee frequently, keep a reusable mug on you.

Buy cotton buds with paper stems and never flush plastic ones down the toilet.

Avoid using face washes and toothpaste with "polypropylene" or "polyethylene" in the ingredients list.

Buy food in bulk and store it in reusable containers.

Use a razor with blades that you re-sharpen from time to time.

Make a conscious effort to buy items which come in cardboard boxes, as they are easier to recycle.

Buy loose fruit and fresh bread to cut out plastic packaging.

Use bars of soap instead of liquid hand wash.

Always take bags-for-life out with you if you're going shopping.

Buy second-hand furniture and equipment and donate items you don't use to charity.

Pack your lunch in reusable containers.

Use reusable microfibre cloths with a tiny bit of water for picking up dust and dirt particles instead of plastic-packaged cleaning products.

Create homemade cleaning products and re-use the bottles once empty – lots of ideas can be found on the internet.

Stop using plastic drinking straws.

Chew mints instead of gum.

* If you have a spare weekend day, offer to help on a beach clean to see first-hand how much rubbish washes ashore, from large plastic containers to tiny nurdles (plastic pellets, which are used in the pharmaceutical industry and ingested by marine life).

CONCLUSION
Living a Balanced Life

Let's hope this book has brought some balance to your life. It may feel a little overwhelming to have absorbed so many ideas and ways to make changes, but you don't have to do them all at once. Pick a couple of things that interest you per week and if you think they are making a positive difference, stick with them and try to add a couple more. If you think you have bitten off more than you can chew, try out other less time-consuming suggestions from the book. Once you get the hang of rewarding yourself with some me-time (it can feel weird at first!), you can always dip back into the book for more inspiration. Adopting a balanced lifestyle will always be a work in progress, but as long as you are striving for a routine that includes your well-being, you will feel a lot happier, healthier and more relaxed.

IMAGE CREDITS

If you're interested in finding out more about our books, find us on Facebook at **Summersdale Publishers** and follow us on Twitter at **@Summersdale**.

www.summersdale.com